EDDIE GRANT

BASEBALL AND THE GREAT WAR

KAREN MARKOE

Karen Markoe

FORT SCHUYLER PRESS

New York 2022

Copyright © 2022 by Karen Markoe
All Rights Reserved
Library of Congress Control Number: 2022948671

Identifiers: LSCCN (print)/ebook
ISBN Number 978-0-9899394-4-7 (hardcover)
ISBN Number 978-0-9899394-3-0 (ebook)
Subjects: LCSH

Printed in United States
First Edition

Cover and book design by Asya Blue Design

Fort Schuyler Press
State University of New York
Maritime College
Bronx, New York 10465

To my father who taught me to love baseball

and

*my teachers at
Christopher Columbus High School in the Bronx,
Hunter College, and Columbia University,
who taught me to love history.*

> "Whoever wants to know the heart and mind of America had better learn baseball, the rules, and reality of the game."

Historian Jacques Barzun
God's Country and Mine: A Declaration of Love, Spiced with a Few Harsh Words
(1954)

> "War is Hell."

General William Tecumseh Sherman
Michigan Military Academy Address
(1879)

ACKNOWLEDGMENTS

Among my colleagues at the State University of New York Maritime College, Sandra Dennis-Hunt and Ira Breskin deserve special thanks. Also librarians and staff at the Franklin, MA Public Library, Harvard College, the National Baseball Hall of Fame, and the National Portrait Gallery in Washington, DC, provided important resources. My thanks to Superintendent Bruce Malone of the American Battle Monuments Commission. Heartful thanks to my Belgian cousin, Diane Solon, who accompanied me to the Meuse-Argonne and served as my guide. Karen Kubala generously shared letters from her relative, Eddie Grant. I appreciate the generosity of The Henry Luce Foundation. My husband, Arnie Markoe, was supportive throughout.

I included photographs and other pictorial representations from *The History of The Seventy Seventh Division August 25th, 1917 - November 11th, 1918* that was designed and written in the field in France, copyright 1919, by the 77th Division Association, New York.

TABLE OF CONTENTS

Preface		i
Introduction		vii
Chapter I	Eddie Grant: The Short and Meaningful Life of an Uncommon Baseball Player	1
Chapter II	Baseball and the Great War	11
Chapter III	Baseball in the Dead-Ball Era	19
Chapter IV	Camp Plattsburgh	23
Chapter V	Camp Upton	29
Chapter VI	The 77th Goes to War	37
Chapter VII	The Lost Battalion	45
Chapter VIII	The Pandemic and Other Deaths	63
Chapter IX	The Mystery	67
Chapter X	The 1918 World Series and Contemporary Subjects	75
Appendix	The United States 1883 – 1918 The Lifespan of Eddie Grant	81
Further Reading		91

PREFACE

When I am asked for my advice about writing a doctoral thesis, I say, "Find a person of consequence who died young and had good handwriting and write her biography." Of course, as a graduate student, I did not follow my own advice but now, in the waning days of my career teaching history, I did find an interesting person to write about who sadly died at an early age.

I came across this person quite accidentally, or at least my husband did; when on a trip to the Baseball Hall of Fame in Cooperstown, he noticed a picture of Edward L. Grant. "Didn't your grandparents live on Edward L. Grant Highway?" he asked. They did, and as I looked more closely, "Guess what," I said, "Whoever Eddie Grant is, we share a birthday, May 21."

That was enough information to pique my interest, and what I learned fascinated me. Eddie Grant was a baseball player in the early twentieth century. Often called "Harvard Eddie," he was a graduate of both Harvard College and Harvard Law School. He mostly played for National League teams, the last was the New York Giants.

As a child, I had seen the Giants play at the Polo Grounds in upper Manhattan, but as a daughter of the Bronx, I was a devout Yankees fan. The Yankees were in my DNA. Nevertheless, I wanted to know more.

Grant was not a great baseball player, but he was good, and a decent human being who respected the English language. He was also nicknamed, "I have it Eddie," because "I got it" just did not sound right to him when camped under an infield pop-up.

During World War I, Grant, too old to be drafted, volunteered to serve. No other major league ballplayer with a prominent career in the majors died in battle. When Eddie Grant was killed in an attempt to rescue the soldiers of the "Lost Battalion," he was 35 years old.

There is also a mystery connected to Grant. The New York Giants had erected a monument in his honor, the only one on the field in the Polo Grounds. On September 29, 1957, the bronze plaque disappeared on the last day the Giants played in the Polo Grounds. There are myths connected to its whereabouts, but maybe a reader of this book will help locate the plaque and the story will be complete.

Now that I live in Manhattan I spend a lot of time walking in Central Park. I stumbled, literally stumbled, on tablets in what was once a grove of oak trees in memory of the soldiers who were killed in Eddie Grant's 307th Regiment, 77th Division. There was his name on the Company H tablet, aged but readable, Captain E.L. Grant, and also on a rock with a bronze plaque and the names of those killed in the Argonne in the final offensive of the war.

My research about Harvard Eddie took me to Grant's hometown of Franklin, MA, to Harvard College, and finally to the Argonne Forest. On that trip, I stopped at war memorials and visited the beautiful American cemetery where Eddie Grant and more than 14,000 American soldiers are buried. It was a moving experience visiting the grave of a man who I never met. He gave his name to my grandparent's street in the West Bronx. He was a captain of a company of mostly immigrant soldiers from New York City who fought for their adopted home, and who revered the man who led them.

I visit the Central Park memorial where I see his name, to walk among the worn tablets, and remember Eddie Grant who gave his life in the final days of the Great War.

Karen Markoe

War memorial plaques, Central Park, NY

*307th Infantry stone inscription
"To the dead of the 307th Infantry A.E,
500 officers and men 1917 – 1918"
Central Park, NY*

INTRODUCTION

The following pages are part social history, part military history. They focus on the life and death of one baseball player and soldier, Edward L. Grant. He lived at a time in the United States when baseball and the military were segregated. Both are part of this book, as are other events that helped define the early twentieth century.

The spark that began the Great War in Europe on June 28, 1914, was the assassination of the heir to the Austro-Hungarian throne, Archduke Franz Ferdinand. It pitted the Central Powers, Germany, Austria-Hungary, the Ottoman Empire, and Bulgaria, against the Allied nations, France, Great Britain, and Russia. At the outset neutral, the United States would eventually be drawn into this long war. Its entry proved decisive.

In September 1914, trench warfare at the First Battle of the Marne resulted in a horrific number of deaths on both sides. However, a quick German victory in the west, envisioned in Germany's Schlieffen Plan, was thwarted by France. A different outcome would have allowed Germany to then turn east to an anticipated longer war with Russia. Eventually, on the western front, both sides faced each other in 400 miles of trenches that extended from the North Sea to the Swiss border.

The sinking of the British passenger ship, the RMS *Lusitania*, on May 7, 1915, with the loss of 1,200 lives, including 128 Americans, made many young men eager to join the war on the side of the Allies. But for another two years, life in the United States went on as usual. Baseball was not interrupted. When Eddie Grant joined the New York Giants in 1913, he earned the princely sum of $3,300, more than Babe Ruth earned when he signed with the Boston Red Sox in 1914. Grant would continue to play baseball through the 1915 season. His last game was on October 6, 1915.

With war very much in the news, President Woodrow Wilson ran for a second term on a "He kept us out of war" platform. However, he understood that with the continuing threat of German submarine warfare, he might not be able to keep the United States out of the fighting. On May 4, 1916, in response to U.S. pressure, Germany issued the Sussex Pledge. It would not target passenger ships, and would allow for the removal of crews of merchant ships carrying war materials before sinking the ships. Meanwhile, the longest battle of the war, the Battle of Verdun, a German offensive, would last over 300 days. The loss of life on both sides was appalling, but in the end, French troops were able to repulse the German invaders.

On February 1, 1917, Germany resumed unrestricted submarine warfare, knowing that it would bring the United States into the war. The calculation would prove Germany's undoing. As the United States was unprepared for war, German military leaders believed the United States would lack sufficient troop strength to affect the outcome of the war until 1919.

The United States entered the war on April 6, 1917, and shortly thereafter, Eddie Grant became the first former major leaguer to enlist. The first active player was Hank Gowdy, catcher for the Boston Braves. Many young, highly educated men, Grant among them, believed it was their patriotic duty to prepare for conflict. They trained in Plattsburgh,

New York. At the time Eddie Grant was a working lawyer. On June 26, 1917, the first U.S. troops arrived in France. Two months later, Eddie Grant was commissioned as a captain in the 307th Division that trained at Camp Upton in Suffolk County, Long Island, New York.

Not until October 1917 near Nancy, a city about 200 miles east of Paris, were the Americans engaged in trench warfare. The Great War, as it was known at the time, was a new kind of war, with reliance on aircraft, poison gas, mobile heavy artillery, tanks, and trench warfare. It cost millions of lives, civilian as well as military. In addition, beginning in 1918, a pandemic raged worldwide, killing even more millions than the war itself.

The final German offensive of the war during the summer of 1918, pitted an exhausted German army against 1.2 million fresh American troops along with the French in the Second Battle of the Marne. On September 26, the final Allied offensive began in the Meuse-Argonne region of northeast France. Again, the loss of life on both sides was monumental. The German government, knowing the end was near, asked for peace based on President Wilson's Fourteen Points. The armistice was signed on November 11, 1918. Eddie Grant had died in battle just five weeks earlier, in a desperate attempt to rescue the "Lost Battalion."

In the years since his death, Eddie Grant has largely been forgotten, although at war's end many tried to keep his memory alive. On Memorial Day in 1921, a plaque was placed on a granite base in the Polo Ground's deep centerfield. Like his memory, it disappeared when the Giants moved to San Francisco. While duplicates were made, the original has never been found.

A few baseball writers attempted to get Grant admitted to the Baseball Hall of Fame, not on his record as a baseball player, but on the basis of his character and his sacrifice. That was the lofty goal of famed Baseball Commissioner Kennesaw Mountain Landis, who had also been charged with the task of rescuing baseball after the Black Sox scandal of 1919.

Landis wished to insert a character clause as a requisite for entrance into the Hall of Fame, and Grant was his candidate. This was not the plan of the baseball writers who vote on Hall of Fame admission. During the patriotic fervor of the Second World War in 1942, Landis again strongly encouraged Grant's admission. It was a losing cause. Grant received only three of 233 votes the baseball writers cast. They would not induct a .249 lifetime hitter into the hallowed halls of Cooperstown.

Like his fellow soldiers in a war that is too often forgotten, a war that changed the world, Eddie Grant should be remembered and honored.

Karen Markoe

Historical map of American Expeditionary Force

WWI Timeline

1914

- **June 28** — Assassination of Archduke Ferdinand of Austria - Hungary sparks war fever
- **July 28** — World War I begins
- **Sept. 6-12** — First Battle of the Marne. Start of trench warfare

1915

- **May 7** — German U-Boat torpedoes the *Lusitania*

1916

- **Feb. 21-Dec. 18** — Battle of Verdun – longest of the War. France repulses German offensive after 302 days

1917

- **Feb. 1** — Germany resumes unrestricted submarine warfare.
- **April 6** — U.S. enters the war
- **June 26** — First U.S. troops arrive in France
- **Oct. 21** — First U.S. battle of the war involving troops of the American Expeditionary Force

1918

- **July 15-Aug. 6** — Last German offensive: Second Battle of the Marne
- **Sept. 26-Nov. 11** — Meuse - Argonne Offensive: Final Offensive of the war
- **Nov. 11** — Armistice: end of the fighting

CHAPTER I

EDDIE GRANT: THE SHORT AND MEANINGFUL LIFE OF AN UNCOMMON BASEBALL PLAYER

The bare facts of the life of Edward L. Grant are interesting in themselves. He was born on May 21, 1883, in Franklin, Massachusetts. Franklin was and still is a pleasant town in which to grow up. It is now a suburb of Boston. It was named for Benjamin Franklin who donated the books to create what was one of the nation's first public libraries. It was also the birthplace of Horace Mann in 1796, who is credited as the most important early advocate for universal public education and teacher training in the United States.

In the year of Eddie Grant's birth, 1883, Chester A. Arthur was president of the United States. Arthur rose from the vice presidency following the assassination of James Garfield. The Civil Service Act was passed in response to the murder of President Garfield by Charles J. Guiteau, a disappointed office seeker.

*Chester A. Arthur
President of the U.S.
1881-1885*

In 1883, the Brooklyn Bridge opened only after skeptics were convinced it was safe when 21 of P.T. Barnum's circus elephants along with 17 camels crossed its expanse without incident. To put 1883 in international perspective, Italian dictator Benito Mussolini was born that year, as were the writer Franz Kafka, the economist John Maynard Keynes, and the fashion designer Coco Chanel.

Eddie, a tall boy and a gifted athlete, attended public schools in Franklin. He lived in a comfortable Victorian home, perhaps one built by his contractor father who was responsible for building many of the homes in Franklin. He had three siblings: his older brother, George, and two younger sisters, Louise and Florence. After school, Eddie could frequently be found on the playing fields of Dean Academy just across the street from his house.

*Eddie Grant's home in
Franklin, MA, across from
Dean Academy's baseball field*

Dean Academy (now Dean College)

Once out of high school in 1901, Eddie enrolled in Dean Academy where he prepared for entrance to Harvard College. His records at Dean indicated that Eddie Grant was a serious student. Almost all his grades were 90s in a rigorous academic program. He was particularly adept at languages; his highest marks were in German and Greek. In fact, the only grade he earned below 90 was an 88 in elocution, perhaps reflecting a certain shyness on the part of this modest young man.

In 1902, Grant matriculated at Harvard College. He played on the freshman baseball team, and as a sophomore hoped to play for the varsity. However, he was declared ineligible because of a summer job he once held. Eddie had played for a minor league club, earning all of forty dollars. While still an undergraduate, he had his first taste of the majors in Cleveland. In the same year in two games at second base, he substituted for the injured future Hall of Famer, player-manager, Napoleon Lajoie.

He also played basketball for Harvard during his freshman and sophomore years. Upon graduation in 1906 Eddie enrolled in Harvard Law School. During his three years studying law, he played minor league baseball during summer vacations.

Once out of law school, he signed with the Milford Club, a semi-professional team in Lynn, Massachusetts. After tryouts for many minor league teams, he signed with the Jersey City Club of the Eastern League. Eddie, with a .322 average, led the league in batting.

At the time, Grant stood at 5 feet 11 inches and weighed 187 pounds. His most prominent features were his ears that stuck out of a pleasant, open face. There are many surviving likenesses of Grant, some on baseball trading cards often found in cigarette packs. Ironically, existing images of Grant do not show him with a cigarette, only show him smoking a pipe. He batted lefty, threw righty, was a gifted fielder, and usually played third base, the so-called "hot corner." He had a strong arm for the long throw to first, and a fast release to second to start the double play.

Beginning in 1907, he played for the Philadelphia Phillies for four seasons. His best major league season was in 1909 when the 26-year-old amassed 170 hits. In that year, only one other National League player, Larry Doyle of the New York Giants had more hits. And while not a consistent hitter throughout his career, Grant was always a fine bunter. As a major leaguer, he played in 992 games. He was popular with both his teammates and the public.

On sports pages Grant was often referred to as "Harvard Eddie Grant," but he was also known as "I have it Eddie." When camped under a pop-up, he would not call out, "I've got it," as most ballplayers of his era would. To his educated ear, "I have it," sounded right.

During the 1909 season, before a doubleheader, Eddie Grant had his most notable day in professional baseball. He found a domino with seven dots and humorously predicted he would get seven hits that day against the New York Giants. Never mind that the team was up against two future Hall of Fame pitchers, Christy Mathewson and Rube Marquard. Surprisingly everyone, including himself, in the opener against the Giants, Grant had five hits against Mathewson. Then, in the second game during his first two times at bat, he had another two hits, this time against Marquard. Grant remained modest, and later noted that he did not get another hit off Mathewson for the rest of the season.

Some years later, in 1925, Mathewson would become a casualty of the Great War, although he was never in combat. At age 38, Mathewson had volunteered to serve in the military, was assigned to a chemical warfare division, and was accidentally gassed during training. His lungs were permanently damaged. Christy Mathewson died of his injury at age 45.

In 1910, still playing with Philadelphia, Grant had another good season. He played in 152 games that season, had 155 hits, and stole 25 bases. His batting average was .268.

Grant makes a play at third.

Nevertheless, that fall he was traded to the Cincinnati Reds. But the most momentous event for Grant that year was that he met a young woman and fell in love. Their chance encounter was in a drug store in Philadelphia where the clerk introduced him to an attractive customer, a 20-year-old woman named Irene Soest. Despite misgivings by Irene's mother who did not like the idea of her daughter being courted by a baseball player, even though a Harvard-educated attorney, the courtship continued. On Christmas Day of that year, Eddie presented Irene with a diamond ring. They were married the following February in the chapel where Irene had taught Sunday school.

Sadly, the marriage was short-lived. On November 25, 1911, on the day that Eddie and Irene had planned to attend the Harvard-Yale football game, Irene awoke complaining of pain in her chest. She died in Eddie's arms that same day, a bride of eight months. She was 21 years old. Irene's heart had probably been damaged when she contracted typhoid fever as a child. Grant rarely talked about Irene after her death, and most people who knew him after that time did not know that he had ever been married. Once, while in the army, he revealed this to his buddy, Major DeLancey Jay, and showed Jay Irene's photograph that Eddie always carried.

Prior to Irene's death, in the 1911 baseball season, Eddie had a disappointing year at the plate. His batting average was just .223. The following year, 1912, he played in only 96 games for Cincinnati, and hit a mere .239.

Grant had entered Harvard as an undergraduate in 1902, the same year that the notorious Andrew Freedman sold the New York Giants that he had first purchased in 1895. Before doing so, however, he brought manager John McGraw to the Giants from Baltimore where Freedman had been the principal owner of the Orioles.

Andrew Freedman is best known as the millionaire Tammany Hall insider who was largely responsible for the construction of the 4, 5, and 6 New York City subway lines in the early 20th century. He was also the founder of the Andrew Freedman House on the Grand Concourse in the Bronx, built as an elegant retirement home for wealthy individuals who had fallen on hard times. The magnificent landmarked building is less than a mile from what is now incongruously named the Edward L. Grant "Highway," formerly Boscobel Avenue, in the Highbridge neighborhood in the West Bronx. While the street near Yankee Stadium was named for Grant in 1945, he never played ball in the stadium. "The House that Ruth Built," opened in the Bronx in 1923. The Polo Grounds in Manhattan where Grant played for the Giants, was only a short distance across the Harlem River from where the current Yankee Stadium sits. The top of Yankee Stadium could be seen from the Polo Grounds.

In 1913, the New York Giants bought Grant's contract from Cincinnati. Manager John McGraw used Grant as a bench coach and an occasional utility infielder. In 1913, Grant played in 27 games for the Giants when they won the National League pennant for the third straight season, and Grant took part in his only World Series. He made appearances as both a pinch-hitter and a pinch-runner in a losing effort as Connie Mack's Philadelphia Athletics beat the Giants four games to one. In the next season, 1914, Grant played in 88 games and had 78 hits for a .277 batting average. In 1915, his final season, he had 40 hits for a .208 average in 87 games. Grant's lifetime batting average was .249.

Eddie Grant, known as easy-going and kind, was the antithesis of his manager who had a well-deserved reputation as tyrannical, difficult in the extreme, with unsavory and criminal associations. John McGraw was alleged to have fixed games and bribed umpires but was never formally charged. McGraw, however, was an enormously successful manager, leading the Giants to ten National League pennants including three World Series victories over his 30 years at the helm. McGraw, himself, a former standout third baseman with the Baltimore Orioles, appreciated Harvard Eddie. Grant played the kind of baseball that McGraw encouraged, essentially small ball – bunt, steal, hit and run.

Lefty Eddie Grant

Grant played for McGraw in the misnamed Polo Grounds. The name was a holdover from an earlier park that the Giants played in, which in fact, was a polo field. The new Polo Grounds was in the northern part of Manhattan island. In the spring of 1911, a fire demolished the wooden stadium. Its replacement, a concrete and steel structure, was built on the same site in a matter of months. The engineers were mindful of the great San Francisco earthquake just five years earlier when they chose their building materials. The Polo Grounds where Grant played his final season was well known for its odd dimensions. While the left-field fence was 279 feet from home plate, and the right-field fence 258 feet, centerfield was an enormous 483 feet away. It created a tunnel-like feel to the Polo Grounds. Not being a long-ball hitter, Grant could only wistfully look out at that far-away target. When a memorial to Grant was erected in 1921, it was placed in the farthest reaches of the field, beneath the 483-foot sign.

Fans could easily reach the Polo Grounds by public transportation, paying a nickel for the elevated railway ride to the 155th Street station. Not only Giants fans called the Polo Grounds home. The New York Cubans of the Negro League played ball there in the 1940s, and the football Giants played there for 30 years until 1956, followed by the football Titans – later the Jets - for four years beginning in 1960. When the Mets began as a team in 1962, they spent two seasons at the Polo Grounds until Shea Stadium opened in 1964.

In 1954, Willie Mays made his spectacular catch of Vic Wertz's long drive to center field in the eighth inning of the first game of the World Series. The Giants went on to win the game, and the next three from the dispirited Cleveland Indians, in what would be the Giants' last World Series in the Polo Grounds. Photos of what became known as "The Catch" clearly show the Edward L. Grant memorial plaque beneath the 483-foot sign to the left of Mays (See photo on page 71).

Grant left baseball in 1915 to join a Boston law firm. During his baseball career, he was recognized as a gifted infielder. Grant was less adept at the plate. He was, however, an excellent base runner, and opponents were aware of his threat to steal.

CHAPTER II

BASEBALL AND THE GREAT WAR

At the time, no one called World War I "World War I". The slaughter was so massive, who would conceive that in a mere score of years the world would be at war again? It was *the Great War*, begun on July 28, 1914, following the assassination of Archduke Franz Ferdinand of Austria–Hungary a month earlier.

In the United States, that the national sport was baseball was unchallenged. The American League was born in 1901, joining the older National League that was founded in 1876. There were 16 teams in two leagues. All the teams were in the east or midwest, St. Louis being the farthest west. But baseball was not a new game. Amateur teams played it as far back as the 1830s, and in 1845 Alexander Cartwright created a set of rules for the Knickerbocker Baseball Club. The first World Series was played in 1903.

"Take Me Out to the Ballgame," the anthem of baseball, was written in 1908 by songwriter Jack Norworth. While riding on a New York subway, he saw an advertisement for a baseball game in the Polo Grounds. Norworth had never been to a baseball game, but he captured the ardor of the fans in that simple tune. At the time, Norworth was married to a diva, the famous Nora Bayes. He was her second of five husbands. She recorded and popularized "Take me Out to the Ballgame," and in the same year, "Shine on Harvest Moon." She also recorded many favorites of the Great War era, including George M. Cohan's "Over There."

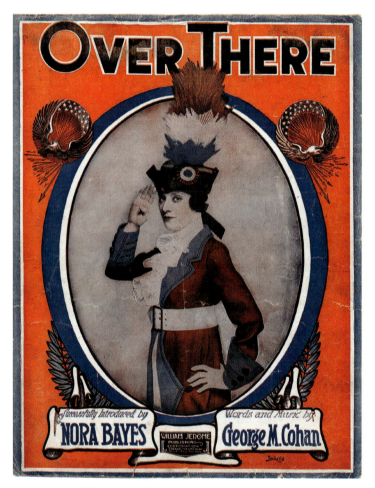

"Over There" – Sheet Music

From April 1917, when the United States entered the war, until the signing of the Armistice on November 11, 1918, baseball remained in the news as fans continued to follow their favorite teams and players. The war did not lessen their enthusiasm for the national pastime. French-born Columbia University professor Jacques Barzun's quote from *God's Country and Mine* is well known, at least half of it is: "Whoever wants to know the heart and mind of America had better learn baseball…" The rest of the quote is: "the rules and realities of the game – and do it by watching first some high school or small-town teams."

America did just that during the first World War, and followed the professional teams as well, often with patriotic fervor, as their baseball heroes trained in camps all over the country, switching their baseball uniforms for the uniforms of the various services.

After the war, most players returned to continue their baseball careers. A few professional ballplayers had died abroad in the service of their country. They were justly recognized by their contemporaries as heroes. The first to be killed on the ground in combat was Captain Edward L. Grant. Two other former major leaguers also died in the Argonne. Each had played in only one major league game, Sergeant Robert "Bun" Troy pitched a single game with the Detroit Tigers in 1912. He died on October 7, 1918, two days after Eddie Grant. The other, Tom Burr, also played in just one major league game, that with the Yankees in 1914. A pilot, Burr died on October 12, 1918, when his plane crashed during training in France.

When Hank Gowdy, the star of the 1914 World Series became the first active player to enlist, it was big news. Fans cheered the Ohioan who had led the Boston Braves in a spectacular come-from-behind season to beat the Philadelphia Athletics four games to one. They applauded Gowdy's patriotism in giving up a lucrative career to fight for the nation as part of the "Rainbow Coalition," made up of National Guard units from various states and Washington D.C. Gowdy was the most famous American to enlist. Only General John Pershing and President Woodrow Wilson were more familiar names to Americans in 1917. When the United States declared war on Germany, Gowdy resigned from the Braves and enlisted in the Ohio National Guard. Sportswriter Grantland Rice immortalized Gowdy in a poem that ended with the line, "That Old Lank Hank was the first to go."

The draft began in stages on June 5, 1917. By September 12, all men between the ages of 18 and 45 had to register. Only once before in U.S. history had there been a draft, and that was during the Civil War. Then men of military age could pay three hundred dollars to avoid the draft, a divisive tactic that had pitted rich against poor. One who did so was Theodore Roosevelt's father, an action that had bothered the younger Roosevelt all of his life. No such buyout was permitted in World War I. Nearly 25 percent of the population signed up, recent immigrants and citizens alike, although only a small percentage actually saw combat. This was a short war for Americans.

Most professional baseball players were deemed fit to serve, and in July 1917 Secretary of War Newton D. Baker, explicitly announced that baseball players of draft age had to assist in the war effort. Criticism was leveled against those identified as slackers, either for not joining up, or for "hiding out" in deferred jobs such as shipbuilding. Of the 320 active players, 20 on each team, 250 served in one capacity or another. Fans across the nation were able to see baseball stars play for the army, navy, marines, or army air service teams, although they were no longer in the big leagues.

Some of the players were African-Americans who as U.S. soldiers had played baseball in the Philippines. They continued to play at a high level during the Great War. Black regiments, such as the legendary Harlem Hellfighters, led in segregated units by white officers, included Negro League stars among their number. One of the most notable was the pitcher, Dick "Cannonball" Redding, a member of the 24th

WW1 Recruiting Poster

Infantry who, like Eddie Grant, had trained at Camp Upton on Long Island. Another was Spottswood Poles, an extraordinary hitter who played in New York for many years with the Lincoln Giants. Called the "Black Ty Cobb," Poles fought alongside the French when he enlisted at 30. The renowned former All-American footballer, performer, and civil-rights activist, Paul Robeson named Poles one of the five greatest Black athletes of all time. Fighting with the 369th Harlem Hellfighters, Poles received five battle stars and the Purple Heart. When he died in 1962, Poles was buried in Arlington National Cemetery.

In Europe, the French army incorporated Black soldiers when white American soldiers refused to fight alongside them. Newspapers carried glowing accounts of the African-American players who heretofore were unknown to most white fans of the game. Overseas in France, Black players helped bring baseball to the French.

Baseball and the military, two sacred U.S. institutions, suffered from the same great stain. Both were segregated. In the years before Jackie Robinson, Black men played professional baseball in the Negro Leagues. But not until 1947 did Black players, Jackie Robinson and Larry Doby break the color line. And not until President Harry Truman, by executive order, desegregated the armed forces, did Black and white soldiers train and fight together. The year was 1948.

When Grant played baseball, most of white America believed that the American and National Leagues were for whites only. And when the draft began in the spring of 1917, it was for all men regardless of color. Eddie Grant trained to become an officer at Camp Plattsburgh, New York when it was closed to men of color, as were 13 other training camps created after the declaration of war.

The number of Black officers was kept at two percent of the total. Segregationists claimed that whites would not fight under Black officers, therefore African-American officers were assigned to command only African-American troops. Segregation was the rule. Black recruits were initially sent to the same camps as whites, Camp Upton among them. Blacks trained both under their own officers, graduates of Howard University and other historically Black colleges, and white officers as well. But opportunities for Blacks in the military were strictly limited, even for those who were college graduates. Typically, Black soldiers worked as stevedores to unload ships, including exceedingly dangerous munition ships, or laborers to build camps or clear roads. Despite racism, they played important roles in the final offensive of the war in the Argonne, but only in segregated units, fighting alongside the French.

Native Americans fared somewhat better, both as baseball players and soldiers. In the Great War, Choctaws and Cherokees pioneered code talking, which became especially important in World War II. When the war began, Native Americans were not citizens of the United States, but citizens of their own tribes. Nevertheless, about 10,000 Native Americans enlisted, and for some, serving in the military was a path to citizenship. Baseball was sometimes tolerant when it came to recruiting Indian players. One was Louis Sockalexis of the Penobscot tribe, nicknamed "The Deerfoot of the Diamond". Reportedly, when the Cleveland Naps were renamed the Cleveland Indians, it was to honor Louis Sockalexis. In 1924, the Indian Citizenship Act mandated citizenship for Native Americans.

CHAPTER III

BASEBALL IN THE DEAD-BALL ERA

Eddie Grant played at a time when the heroes of the game, for the most part, were pitchers. During the "dead-ball" era, home runs were few, as rubber-filled baseballs generally stayed on the playing field. Inside-the-park home runs were more common than balls that cleared the fences unlike during later eras, when sluggers would swing for and reach the seats. In his entire ten-year career in the majors, Grant hit a total of five home runs, four of them inside the park. Playing for Cincinnati, Grant hit two in the same month in 1912. The last in his baseball career was against the great Rube Marquard.

In the dead-ball era, the game stressed strategy. Pitchers were the stars. Ballplayers like Eddie Grant, who could bunt, steal bases, and play excellent defense were also crucial to dead-ball strategy. Power was rarely in the equation until Babe Ruth changed the game and cork cores made the baseball livelier. Ty Cobb, for example, a long-time Detroit Tiger star whose playing days began in 1905 and continued until 1928, had a lifetime batting average of .366, and averaged only five home runs a year. Despite few home runs, baseball's popularity increased during the dead-ball era.

Grant and Cobb never played against each other, as they were in opposing leagues. When the Tigers won the pennant in the three years beginning in 1907, Grant was playing for the Phillies when the Cubs (twice) and the Pirates (once) faced Cobb and the Tigers. We do not know how Grant felt about the well-publicized notorious behavior of Cobb. He was combative on and off the field, carried a pistol, brawled with teammates, opposing players, umpires, and even an occasional fan. The Georgia Peach's personality was the opposite of the genial Eddie Grant, who preferred reading to playing poker with his teammates and was never known to exhibit anything but sportsman-like behavior.

Baseball's popularity rose in the early years of the twentieth century. It continued as America's sport, the national pastime. Women, as well as men, attended games in great numbers, even before they won the right to vote in 1920 with the passage of the 19th amendment to the Constitution. It was a respectable thing for women to do at a time when they faced severe cultural and legal limitations. In 1910, when President William Howard Taft threw out the first ball of the season, it exemplified the nationwide acceptance of the game. That began a tradition continued by most presidents, including Taft's successor, Woodrow Wilson, even during the Great War years. Only presidents Jimmy Carter and Donald Trump did not follow. Carter, however, threw out the first ball in the seventh game of the 1979 World Series between the Pittsburgh Pirates and the Baltimore Orioles.

President Woodrow Wilson throwing out the first pitch on Opening Day, 1916

Children and grown men played baseball in sandlots and pastures across the country. In New York City, small spaces were found along piers and in spacious Central Park. In cities everywhere, empty lots were set aside for ballfields, an outgrowth of the playground movement led mostly by women during the Progressive Era. Their numbers included Jane Addams of Hull House fame in Chicago, and Lillian Wald of the Henry Street Settlement in Manhattan. They advocated the benefits of team sports for the healthy growth of children.

The equivalent of bubblegum baseball cards of a later era, pictures of ballplayers were tucked into cigarette packs, strange collectibles for children. Eddie Grant's image with his distinctive jug ears could be found on several of these cigarette trading cards.

Fans attended baseball games by the thousands. World War I did not dampen enthusiasm for the national pastime. Secretary of War Newton Baker championed team sports as an alternative to less savory pursuits for young males.

American troops continued to play baseball in Europe, even as they also followed their favorite teams back home in the pages of *The Sporting News* or the military newspaper, *Stars and Stripes*. In 1917, there was little disruption of the baseball schedule. In 1918, however, the regular baseball season was shortened by 23 to 31 games, depending on the team. Secretary Baker allowed the 1918 World Series to take place after the regular season. That World Series was played between the Boston Red Sox and the Chicago Cubs. The Red Sox won the Series that year, behind the pitching of Babe Ruth. It would be 86 years before the Red Sox would win another World Series.

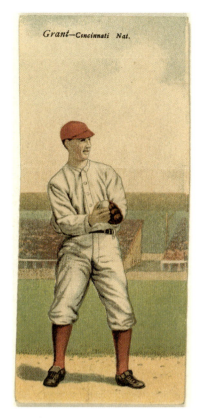

Eddie Grant's image on a cigarette trading card

As a war measure to conserve fuel, the country went on Daylight Savings Time in March 1918. It was first adopted by Germany and Austria in 1916, then by America's allies in 1917. The Standard Time Act was unpopular in the United States, and Congress repealed it just seven months later. President Wilson vetoed the repeal, but Congress overrode the president's veto and daylight savings time was re-enacted only during World War II.

CHAPTER IV

CAMP PLATTSBURGH

Camp Plattsburgh, a military training site, to prepare officers for war was primarily the brainchild of Dr. Leonard Wood, a graduate of Harvard Medical School, and commanding officer of Theodore Roosevelt and the Rough Riders in Cuba during the Spanish-American War. Many of the prospective officers, like Grant, were graduates of Ivy League colleges. They included Theodore Roosevelt's son, Quentin, and Eddie Grant's Harvard Law School classmate, Charles Whittlesey, later to become company commander of the famed Lost Battalion. African-Americans, no matter their education level were not accepted at Camp Plattsburgh during the administration of segregationist Woodrow Wilson.

President Woodrow Wilson

The sinking of the *Lusitania* in May 1915 propelled young professionals, lawyers like Eddie Grant who anticipated eventual U.S. involvement in the war, to become part of Wood's "preparedness movement." The Harvard Club in Manhattan at 35 West 44th Street was the center of operations for Leonard Wood.

When Eddie Grant and his former New York Giants teammate, Elwood "Moose" McCormick, enlisted and were sent to the Officer Candidate School in Plattsburgh, Grant's sense of patriotic humor was on display. He wrote that when his friend McCormick took his physical exam, he had an accident – "for when they took his chest expansion – he broke the tape measure – he expanded seven inches."

McCormick made news in the summer of 1918, when he criticized baseball players for not enlisting, especially lambasting some players who he accused of hiding out in factories producing war materials to avoid serving in Europe. McCormick said that he was voicing the opinions of American soldiers who continue to love the game, but were angered by baseball slackers.

It was not only the ballplayers who enlisted. Shortly after the U. S. entered the war, New York Yankees co-owner 50-year-old Captain T L Huston, enlisted in the 16th Army Engineer Corps. He had first served as a 21-year-old in the Spanish-American War. In 1917, he was sent to France and rose to full colonel. Huston was infuriated by ballplayers who sat out the war in shipyards, rather than fighting the Germans. When Huston retired from the Yankees in 1923, he became the Commander of Veterans of Foreign Wars (VFW).

Prior to Eddie Grant going to Plattsburgh, Theodore Roosevelt had visited the camp where he spoke out against "hyphenates." Roosevelt's meaning was apparent, even though so much of the fighting force consisted of patriotic immigrants who had eagerly signed up to fight for their adopted country. This was especially true of many recruits at Camp Upton on Long Island, New York where Eddie Grant would later be stationed.

The Plattsburgh men trained hard, but after hours one of the most popular leisure activities was baseball. Having Eddie Grant, a former major leaguer in their games, must have meant a great deal to those officers in training. Grant was well liked, respected, and admired for his modesty and wit.

Theodore Roosevelt
President of the U.S. 1901-1909

The Plattsburgh volunteers were influenced by Theodore Roosevelt, his intellect, dedication to the strenuous life, and intense patriotism. Undoubtedly, most recruits agreed with the former president that the United States should have entered the war in Europe earlier than it had. In 1916, Democrat Woodrow Wilson ran on the rallying cry, "He kept us out of war." Like Roosevelt, Plattsburgh men were largely Republicans, and many like Theodore Roosevelt, had great antipathy for Democrats. In turn, many Democrats were uncomfortable in the company of the Republican elite.

On May 18, 1917, the Selective Service Act required all men between the ages of 21 to 30 to register with local draft boards, the first draft since the Civil War. "Harvard Eddie" Grant was 33 when war broke out, too old to be drafted, but not too old to fight. Only later in the war was the draft extended to age 45 when more manpower was required. In June, the initial wave of soldiers arrived in Saint-Nazaire on the west coast of France.

During World War I, baseball was played by servicemen, wherever they found themselves. Bases and ships had their own teams, and rivalries were intense. The fortunate teams had professional ballplayers in their ranks. Eddie Grant was a welcome presence at Camp Plattsburgh when he volunteered for service in the spring of 1917.

In a letter to his younger sister Florence, Eddie, or Les, as his family called him, wrote how he applied for a commission in the Officers Reserve Corps, ORC. And exhibiting a bit of whimsy, he added, "The martial spirit of the Grants was found to assert itself." In the same letter, he urged his sister to not let her husband Earle "get foolish." Grant said, "There are enough fellows in my position without others." That is, Grant had nobody dependent on him while his brother-in-law headed a household that included a wife, two children, and Eddie's father. Grant was adamant. "I cannot make this too strong – his garden and work are enough." Grant used a baseball metaphor in his attempt to reassure his family about the war. He wrote:

> *I am not the least bit pessimistic about this and can't see why any of you should be. Why the Germans won't be able to win a game from us. We would knock old Hinderburg (sic) out of the box in the first inning.*

Eddie Grant assured his family that he would do "all the fighting for all of us."

On August 15, Eddie Grant was commissioned a captain in the 307th Infantry in the 77th Liberty Division. Two silver bars identified his rank as that of captain. Members of the 77th sported a shoulder patch of the Statue of Liberty.

Shoulder patch of 77th Liberty Division

CHAPTER V

CAMP UPTON

The United States stayed out of the Great War for three years, but when Germany announced a resumption of unrestricted submarine warfare early in 1917, President Wilson asked Congress for a declaration of war. On April 6, 1917, the United States entered the conflict against Germany. However, involvement in the war for some Americans had begun earlier. Thousands enlisted in the CEF, the Canadian Expeditionary Force, and others went to England and France to fight against Germany. Before the American entry, bankers, most notably J. P. Morgan, had loaned millions of dollars to the signatories of the Entente Cordiale, Great Britain and France, allowing them to purchase munitions and other supplies for the war effort.

Anti-German sentiments intensified when a German submarine sank the British passenger ship *RMS Lusitania* on May 7, 1915, off the coast of Ireland with the loss of 1,198 lives including 128 Americans. The German government had warned travelers that "Vessels flying the flag of Great Britain or any of her allies are liable to destruction." It had placed ads in many American newspapers, but they were not always heeded. Following a public outcry, schools stopped offering German language courses; the Metropolitan Opera in New York City no longer staged works by Wagner and other German composers. Sauerkraut became "liberty cabbage." German measles was known as "liberty measles."

The RMS Lusitania of the Cunard Line

Eddie Grant's generation was a half-century removed from the Civil War. Most young men had not experienced war firsthand and were certainly unfamiliar with the new weapons of war: poison gas, tanks, flame throwers, high explosive shells, airplanes, and heavy artillery.

Grant graduated from Camp Plattsburgh with distinction and the rank of captain. He was assigned to Company H, New York's 307th Infantry 77th Division at Camp Upton. Created in the summer of 1917, in rural Yaphank, Suffolk County, Long Island, Camp Upton was about sixty miles east of Manhattan. Grant's good friend and fellow Harvard Law School classmate, Major Charles Whittlesey, like most of the newly minted officers from Plattsburgh, was also assigned to Camp Upton. Barely a year later, Eddie Grant's attempt to rescue the surrounded Major Whittlesey and his troops led to Grant's death.

Good Old Camp Upton Days

View of Camp Upton

The 77th Ready for Overseas Service

Camp Upton in winter

The Camp Upton recruits reflected the population of New York City, predominantly immigrants or the children of immigrants. Unlike their officers, these soldiers typically were Irish, Italians, Jews, Poles, and Greeks. Thirty thousand men trained at Camp Upton, now the site of Brookhaven National Laboratory. Many were from the Lower East Side, Harlem, and Brooklyn. Once an independent city, Brooklyn had been the third-largest in the United States, until it became part of New York City on January 1, 1898.

One of their number at Camp Upton was Israel Baline, a Russian-born songwriter, who had changed his name to Irving Berlin. Having written Alexander's Ragtime Band in 1911, he was already celebrated as the "King of Tin Pan Alley." Drafted at age 29, Berlin wrote the unofficial national anthem, "God Bless America," while at Camp Upton. He kept that music score in his song trunk for 20 years, until Kate Smith sang it in public for the first time on Armistice Day in 1938. Based on his months at Camp Upton, he also wrote the comedic, "Oh How I Hate to Get Up in the Morning," with the memorable line, "Someday I'm going to murder the bugler, someday they are going to find him dead." Like Eddie Grant, Irving Berlin lost a young wife months after their marriage. Her death was from typhoid fever, possibly a contributing cause of Eddie Grant's wife's death as well.

New York City played an important role in the First World War. Wall Street loaned money to the Allies, and once the war was declared, Liberty Bonds were sold on the streets. Film stars including Charlie Chaplin, Douglas Fairbanks, and Mary Pickford, raised funds for the war effort. The great port of New York was the major embarkation point of troops bound for Europe. And recognizing the centrality of New York to the war effort, German submarines patrolled the waters close to its shores. Anti-German feelings were not confined to New York, but as the center of the newspaper world, what was written in New York City greatly influenced attitudes in other parts of the country.

Eddie Grant's 77th called itself the "Metropolitan Division," reflecting that the recruits were almost exclusively from metropolitan New York City. African-Americans, who were to make Harlem their home in the following decade, were segregated in their own division, the 15th National Guard Unit. They trained in Peekskill, New York about 45 miles north of Manhattan. These soldiers helped build Fort Dix in New Jersey, as well as Camp Upton on Long Island.

Formed in 1916, the 15th National Guard Unit faced intense discrimination, despite the patriotism that impelled African-Americans to enlist. With no acceptance by white soldiers, the 15th was sent to France, where General Philippe Pétain, "Hero of the Battle of Verdun" convinced General John J. "Black Jack" Pershing, commander of the American Expedition Force (AEF), to allow Black soldiers to train and fight alongside the French army on the Western Front. Ultimately, Black soldiers served longer on the front lines than white American soldiers. The African-Americans were welcomed by the French. That appreciation was not the case when the soldiers returned to a segregated society in the United States.

African-American Soldiers Prepare for War

On July 28, 1917, the still-young National Association for the Advancement of Colored People, NAACP, founded in 1909 on the centennial of Abraham Lincoln's birth, organized a silent march down Fifth Avenue. It was to protest a barbaric riot against African-Americans in East St. Louis, Illinois, as well as lynchings in Waco, Texas, and Memphis, Tennessee. Known as the "silent parade," 10,000 African-Americans marched from 57th Street to Madison Square at 23rd Street. The NAACP leadership reminded the nation that Black soldiers had served in every war from the American Revolution to 1916 when Black Buffalo Soldiers fought under General Pershing in Mexico to pursue Pancho Villa. The Great War would be no different as African-American soldiers confined in segregated units comprised nearly 10 percent of all recruits.

The 15th was only one of many National Guard regiments from New York. Perhaps the best known was the Fighting 69th. In August 1917, 2,100 guardsmen of the 69th said goodbye to New York as they paraded in the Polo Grounds. Then it was off to France. Immortalized for his service, Father Francis P. Duffy was chaplain of the 69th. A statue in the northern section of Times Square, named for Father Duffy, is a reminder for tourists and New Yorkers alike of his heroism.

From various accounts, we know that while the New York recruits learned to become soldiers, they were hampered in several ways. Many did not speak English, and some with German backgrounds, had conflicted feelings about the fatherland. For others, army life was an unwelcome interruption of civilian careers.

The recruits began to arrive at Camp Upton by rail in September 1917. In the days and the months of basic training, the men were indoctrinated into army life, inoculated for diphtheria and typhus, and issued uniforms, mess kits, and blankets. They were questioned about their special skills, including languages spoken, and work history.

Following a week of drilling, on Saturday afternoons soldiers were allowed to take the train to Manhattan, the last one returning back on the 2:59 a.m., known as the "Owl." In December, they were granted time off to celebrate Christmas and New Year's Eve. On February 22, Washington's birthday, Eddie Grant's 77th paraded up 5th Avenue. This was "New York's Own," with its insignia, the Statue of Liberty worn as a shoulder patch. After their training at Camp Upton these New York men had turned into a formidable fighting force. The war was beginning to intensify for U.S. troops, and New York newspapers reported the first death of U.S. soldiers in November 1917.

CHAPTER VI

THE 77ᵀᴴ GOES TO WAR

In 1917 the United States was unprepared for war, and transporting troops and supplies across the Atlantic to fight a war in Europe was a mammoth undertaking. There were not enough U.S. ships for the job, but vital assets remained in the port of New York and had been there since the war began in August 1914. Eighteen German merchant ships had been berthed in the United States, then a neutral country. The U.S. seized the ships on April 6, 1917. Unattended and rusting for three years, they were in need of major repairs. Miraculously, the ships took only five months to be overhauled and refitted, despite early estimates that the work would take at least two years. These ships subsequently were used to ferry some 200,000 U.S. soldiers to the European war. Perhaps the best-known ship was the former *Vaterland,* renamed the *Leviathan* under U.S. flag. Not all the ships required renaming, as before the war many had been built for the U.S. tourist trade including the *George Washington*, *President Lincoln,* and *Amerika.* To avoid the fate of ships that were previously sunk by German U-boats, beginning in March 1918, ships were dazzle painted.

It was the idea of British artist, Norman Wilkinson. A dazzle-painted ship's exact position was difficult to calculate when viewed through a periscope.

The Division that took the stingers off Kaiser Bill

On April 6, 1918, the first anniversary of the U.S. entry into the war, a segment of the 77th Division left Camp Upton by train for Long Island City in the county of Queens. From there, ferries took the soldiers around the Battery in Lower Manhattan to the Hudson River. At Pier 59 on West 18th Street they met the British troopship *SS Justicia*, at the time the fifth largest vessel in the world. It would carry them to Europe. In Roman mythology, *Justicia* is the daughter of Zeus and Themis. Originally built for the Holland America line as the *SS Statendam*, the British government acquired the ship when the war began. The *Justicia* was operated by the White Star Line. Its best-known ship was the *RMS Titanic* that went down on April 15, 1912 approximately 400 miles off the coast of Newfoundland after hitting an iceberg on its maiden voyage.

Built for the ocean tourist trade in Belfast, Northern Ireland, the *SS Justicia* was meant to carry 800 first-class passengers, 600 second-class passengers, and 2,030 third-class passengers, but as a troopship it sometimes packed in more than 5,000 soldiers. The 77th Liberty

Division, passing its namesake, the Statue of Liberty, began its voyage from New York City to Liverpool, by way of Halifax, Nova Scotia.

The *SS Justicia* was 776 feet long and housed soldiers below deck where their hammocks were strung over mess tables. The men wore life preservers day and night as the ship sailed northward toward Halifax. The city of Halifax had been largely destroyed on December 6, 1917, by a collision of two ships, one a fully loaded munition ship destined for Europe. The explosion killed more than 1,900 people, injured as many as 9,000 more and leveled much of Halifax. At the time it was the largest man-made explosion ever recorded.

On July 30, 1916, unlike the accident of the Halifax explosion, there was an earlier example of a massive explosion, this time on U.S. territory even before Congress declared war. Reportedly, German saboteurs set off an explosion on Black Tom Island in New York Harbor. It registered 5.5 on the Richter Scale. Barges and cars of the Lehigh Valley Railroad filled with munitions and dynamite to be shipped to the Allies were destroyed. Windows in nearby Brooklyn and Manhattan shattered and four people died. It damaged the torch of the Statue of Liberty on nearby Bedloe's (now Liberty) Island. The explosion was widely reported in the press. It certainly would have been known to Eddie Grant.

Leaving Halifax on April 9, as part of a convoy of ten passenger and cargo ships ringed by U.S. and British escort ships, the *SS Justicia* made its way to England. Twice a day the men engaged in lifeboat drills. The Halifax to Liverpool leg took two weeks. Despite camouflage dazzle paint, the *SS Justicia* had a short life. On its way back to New York from Belfast, she was sunk three months later on July 19, 1918 by German submarines UB-64 and UB-124. Sixteen crew members died in the attack.

After two weeks at sea with no serious threats from German submarines, the *SS Justicia* arrived in Liverpool, where the soldiers disembarked and boarded trains to Dover. Eddie Grant and his men then transferred to a yacht that served as a ferry to cross the English Channel to Calais, a trip of an hour and thirty-five minutes. The ferry had been the yacht of Bavarian-born Belgian Queen Elisabeth before the war. Arriving in Calais, the soldiers could hear the sounds of German bombs and British anti-aircraft guns, but suffered no casualties. They also saw for the first time the results of devastation from the war in the port city of Calais, shelled a week earlier. The reality of war began to sink in for the young soldiers. The troops were issued gas masks and helmets, and their American Springfields were exchanged for the lighter British Enfields. The men of the 77th then loaded onto French boxcars, many fitted out for 40 men and eight horses.

Arrival of American soldiers watched by German POWs

General Pershing had strict guidelines for deploying his army. Troops were to be trained, ideally for six months in the United States, an additional two months in France, then another month in battle, in less than trying conditions. They were to serve only under American officers, with the exception of African-American soldiers. Black troops had arrived in France in December 1917 to serve under French command. When they reached the port city of Brest, they charmed French onlookers with a jazz rendition of La Marseillaise.

African-American soldiers learning French

In the campaign against Germany, the 77th first worked with the British Army in May and early June around Calais, and then moved by train to the Baccarat sector in the province of Lorraine. In this sector where "the front was quiet" and allowed for training with the French, the Fourth of July and Bastille Day were both celebrated. The next phase for the American troops was along the River Vesle where there was heavy fighting in August and early September. An account of the 77th described the Vesle in the following words:

Soldiers' ball game with YMCA equipment

CHAPTER VII

THE LOST BATTALION

Until 1918, American Doughboys, Grant included, saw little action. Marshal Ferdinand Foch, Supreme Allied Commander, attempted to get Pershing's troops to fight under French command, but Pershing, backed by President Wilson, resisted Foch's demands. Not until the summer of 1918 was an agreement reached, brokered in part by French Marshal Philippe Pétain. White American troops would fight under U.S. command, rather than become part of the French army. It is worth mentioning that in another part of the world at the same time, in September 1918, it would not be the case. There U.S. troops fought under British command in Siberia against the Bolsheviks in the Russian civil war. In that theater, five thousand U.S. doughboys fought for ten months during the winter of 1918-1919, where more than two hundred lost their lives.

On August 31, Eddie Grant wrote a letter to his father. His comments on the war were designed to keep his family from worrying. Grant wrote about "a playful shell," two words that rarely appear together. He joked about not being able to go to a store when his trousers were damaged.

Dear father,

Have not had much chance to write lately but take the time to tell you that I'm alright – even if I am very dirty – have no clothes and need a haircut.

My trousers were fine until the other day when I ripped them rolling over the rock of a sunken road to avoid a playful shell they fired at me and an automatic gunner as we were coming across the fields. Me (sic) soon were under a cover but my last pair of trousers were spoiled and can't see just when will get another pair for stores are rather scarce over here.

Fall is in the air – here and guess it sets in rather early – but hear that it does not get so cold as it does in New Hampshire for instance.

Just now we are resting a little – in fact just beginning it and we all hope that it will continue for some time as we are all rather tired – we have not had much sleep lately and the thing that bothered the men most was that for five days they had nothing but canned beef and crackers. They miss hot coffee but now they are getting plenty.

Will expect to hear from you at any time now and will write again soon. And tell Louise and Florence I will write soon – and that they must write me very often.

Best of luck and love to all of you.

With love to all
Your loving son
Les

Les was what his family called him. The "L" in Grant's name stood for Lester. It was the last letter that he sent, and it was less than a month before the battle that would end his life and shortly thereafter end the war.

On September 26, 1918, Americans moved into the Meuse-Argonne sector in the northeastern corner of France, an area of deep woods and gulches pounded by enemy gunfire. It was the final offensive of the war. The terrain was difficult to negotiate and made more difficult by the cold, wet weather. Despite heavy losses, Montfaucon, the Mount of the Falcon, was seized, a major victory for the American troops. The front extended from the Argonne Forest twenty miles to the Meuse River. For six weeks, more than a million French and Americans fought the Germans in the Meuse-Argonne. Artillery caused the most destruction, casualties, and deaths in World War I, and that was especially the case in the Meuse-Argonne campaign. It was fought in the massive Argonne Forest, more than twice the size of the five boroughs of New York City. The combatants included a future U.S. president, Harry S. Truman, a captain in the Missouri National Guard.

There were parallels with Truman, who had volunteered to serve in the guard. Like Eddie Grant, Truman was too old to be drafted, and like Grant, Truman was promoted to captain. Both Grant and Truman fought in the Meuse-Argonne, but there the parallels end. Truman's Battery D suffered no losses, and Truman returned to civilian life and a career in politics. A United States senator, he ran on the Democratic ticket with Franklin Roosevelt for vice-president in 1944. Then became president when F.D.R. died in office in 1945. He was the successful candidate for president in 1948, serving until 1953.

In addition to U.S. forces fighting under Pershing, the Allied attack included the African-American 15th fighting alongside the French. Mostly New Yorkers from Harlem, the 15th National Guard unit was renamed the 369th Infantry Regiment, which became known as the

"Harlem Hellfighters." They earned the nickname in the battle against Germans troops because of the fierceness with which they fought.

Black troops faced discrimination by white Americans on the battlefield as well as back home in the states despite their demonstrated patriotism. They were not invited to be part of the Rainbow Division. Segregationists justified that exclusion by arguing that black was not a color of the rainbow. These Black patriots suffered daily indignities and hardships. They were often sent into battle without adequate training. Sometimes they were denied the Thanksgiving and Christmas rations that white soldiers received. In the Argonne, they were frequently the scapegoats for the failures of their white officers. Black soldiers suffered from exhaustion and lack of food. Material support was often in short supply as when wire cutters were not available to cut through German barbed wire, preventing them from moving forward. At war's end, the French awarded 170 Black soldiers the Croix de Guerre for heroism. In New York City they were honored with a parade up Fifth Avenue.

The victory parade for the 369th, February 1919

Rep. Suozzi at the dedication of the Harlem Hellfighters Monument in Harlem, July 2021

More than a century later, in May 2021, legislation was introduced in the House of Representatives by Congressman Tom Suozzi to award the Congressional Gold Medal to the Harlem Hellfighters. It passed the House of Representatives on June 16 and the Senate on August 9. President Biden signed it into law on August 28, 2021 (PL 117-38).

The German army, at one time considered the finest fighting force in the world, had been entrenched in the region for four years. A century later, the woods are still thick and muddy underfoot. Fragments of barbed wire and spent shells are uncovered by local farmers in the vicinity of the so-called "pocket," where Major Whittlesey and the 308th infantry had been trapped.

Grant was among the first American officers sent to a sector in the Argonne Forest held by five German divisions. The German occupation of the Argonne had been unsuccessfully challenged, but the Argonne was a "mighty door" leading to Germany. In October, Pershing directed his men to advance, an aggressive strategy to purge the Argonne of German troops. That was the goal. Not influenza, a shortage of trucks, or inclement weather, would deter Pershing in his effort to break the German line.

General John Pershing

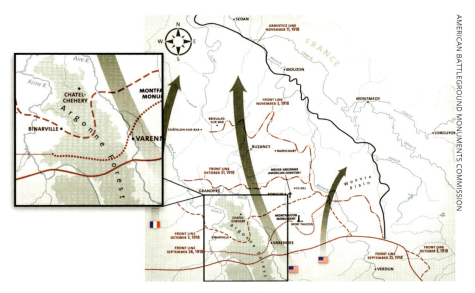

Map of France showing the Meuse-Argonne Forest

Deep in the Argonne Forest, on October 2, Grant's friend Major Charles Whittlesey, and 679 men entered "the pocket" in the Charlevaux Ravine. Virtually no sunlight could break through the forest canopy. It rained constantly. Advancing to an area called Charlevaux Mill, combined companies had shed coats and blankets to press on. Ground communications rapidly broke down. Messages were distorted. At one point, soldiers kept track of each other by putting a hand on the soldier in front. Word sent down the line "Watch out for the holes" emerged at the other end as "Wash out your clothes," like a children's game of telephone, but without a comic outcome. When Whittlesey's troops moved ahead of the Americans on both sides of them, they were surrounded by Germans. Others in the 77th had made repeated attempts to reach them but were unsuccessful. Whittlesey refused to surrender. Each day more men died as they waited to be rescued. Their rescuers suffered heavy losses as well. Grant was just one among many.

Germans strung more barbed wire as the Americans dug funk holes, military jargon for dugouts, where men of the 77th shivered and grew desperate. Twice a day Americans faced attacks by German artillery, machine gunfire, and potato mashers, handheld stick grenades that were first introduced in 1915, and were widely available and effective. The battle lines were drawn close. Complicating matters, English-speaking German soldiers often shouted misleading commands to confuse the Americans. On the first day, Whittlesey's force lost 80 men. After entering "the pocket," trapped men were unable to bury their dead as the suffering continued. They had no food, no water, and no medical supplies. Bandages were removed from the bodies of the dead to serve the living. Major Whittlesey dispatched six carrier pigeons with descriptions of their position. All arrived at headquarters. Allied planes dropped food packages, but they landed tantalizingly out of reach of the isolated soldiers. Numerous failed attempts were made by troops of the 77th to reach the men of the so-called "Lost Battalion," which history records as neither lost nor a battalion.

Major Charles Whittlesey

Grant and reinforcements were sent late in the day on a rainy Saturday, October 5, to rescue Whittlesey's men. Grant was sleep-deprived and sick. A member of his company who was a former policeman at the Polo Grounds, noticed that Grant was too tired to hold a cup of coffee. Still, Grant carried on. Assigned additional command to replace a wounded superior officer, Captain Grant tried to protect his men from an incoming barrage. His last words were "Flop everyone," before being struck by shrapnel that tore through his side. Grant was killed instantly and fell in the mud. We will never know if he was killed by German gunfire, or American or French artillery fire. At the time it was called "friendly barrage."

Knowing of Whittlesey's plight, the Germans made repeated attempts to get the Americans to surrender. Whittlesey was reported to have responded, "Go to Hell." It made for a good story, but Whittlesey, in fact, did not respond at all to their demands. Days later, Abe Kozikowski, a Polish immigrant, volunteered to go for help and succeeded where others who had tried were either killed or captured. Kaz, as he was known, only had arrived in the United States two years before, when he crawled past the Germans under cover of darkness and was able to get help. He led rescuers back to the desperate men, many of whom were severely wounded. Of the 679 who had entered the ravine, only 180 were able to walk out on their own. Just 252 survived, Charles Whittlesey among them. Pershing in his memoirs noted the "deeds of daring" and praised Whittlesey and his men who refused to surrender.

A sad conclusion to the life of Lieutenant Colonel and Congressional Medal of Honor recipient Charles Whittlesey occurred on November 24, 1921. After getting his affairs in order, the hero of the Lost Battalion booked passage on the *SS Taloa* bound for Cuba. Coincidently, the ship's captain was named Grant, Farquhar Grant. The captain invited his distinguished passenger to dine with him at the captain's table, and Whittlesey, reportedly in good spirits, asked Captain Grant to find out the result of the Army-Navy football game. Those who saw Charles

Whittlesey that evening found him cheerful and talkative. But the next morning he could not be located. A search of his stateroom revealed that Whittlesey had left a note. He had committed suicide by jumping off the ship, another casualty of the Great War. He was a thoughtful and sensitive man, a former pacifist, and had suffered emotionally as a result of the Lost Battalion tragedy.

On October 8, 1918, the day that Whittlesey and his men were rescued, Corporal Alvin York, an extraordinary marksman who had honed his skills hunting wild turkeys in his native Pall Mall, Tennessee, singlehandedly killed 25 of the enemy, and captured 132. He was promoted to sergeant, later awarded the Congressional Medal of Honor and became a national hero.

Corporal Alvin York

Battlefield marker

Eddie Grant was first buried where he fell, then reburied in a small cemetery that was originally planned for German war dead in the Argonne. He was eventually reburied in the magnificent Meuse-Argonne American Cemetery.

Eddie Grant's gravesite

Eddie Grant's death, the first professional major league baseball player to die in the Great War, was widely reported in the press. *The New York Times* story title read, "Captain 'Eddie' Grant Killed in France. Ex-Third Basemen of the Giants Slain in Attempt to Rescue Lost Battalion." *The Times* characterized Grant as "a handy utility player who could fill in any position on the infield. While never a heavy hitter, he was a skillful fielder and a smart base runner." The military newspaper, *Stars and Stripes*, reported Grant's death on October 25 under the headline, "Baseball Loses Big League Star in Greater Game." The paper reported that "New York's own," H Company, 307th Division arrived late in the afternoon of the third day that the so-called Lost Battalion was encamped in the mud of the forest floor. It quoted Grant's last words to the men, "Flop everyone," as he led his band of rescuers. Several days later in an interview, Major Whittlesey told reporters, "The real story is with the men who day and night fought their way to our rescue."

The Meuse-Argonne offensive was the deadliest battle in U.S. history. Edward L. Grant was one of 53,402 total U.S. deaths in combat during World War I, and roughly half of those deaths (26,277) were in the Meuse-Argonne. There were nearly 96,000 wounded. The comparative figures at Gettysburg were 7,000 killed, 33,000 wounded, and 11,000 missing, and that counts both sides in the Civil War. The vast majority of World War I combat deaths were able to be identified, as for the first time in a U.S. war, all soldiers were issued "dog tags." It enabled the deceased to be buried with their names inscribed on grave markers.

A century after Eddie Grant attempted to rescue Major Whittlesey and the soldiers of the Lost Battalion, signs of the fighting are everywhere. Small local museums house century-old canteens, shovels, boots, munitions, and the artifacts of four years of the Great War. In fields and surrounding villages, cemeteries and elaborate war memorials, many built in the relatively prosperous 1920s, dot the gently rolling hills. Close inspection reveals tunnels and bunkers from the German occupation. Narrow-gauge train tracks overgrown by vegetation survive, indicated how Germans moved food, munitions, even books, and films underground for four years.

Tourists, mostly French and German, Belgians and Dutch as well, come to Lorraine to pay their respects to their countrymen. Noticeable by their absence are Americans, although occasionally a family will arrive to visit the grave of a deceased ancestor at the impressive and meticulously cared for Meuse-Argonne American Cemetery. It is the resting place of 15,000 American soldiers who perished in the Argonne in the final offensive of the Great War. However, some of the deceased were brought home to their families, like PFC Edward Heusser, a German-American who was killed in the Meuse-Argonne on October 12, 1918 and buried in Woodlawn Cemetery in the Bronx, New York.

In the Meuse-Argonne American Cemetery, Eddie Grant's grave under a plain white cross, can be found with an assist from a computer in the welcome center, directing visitors to Plot A, Row 2, Grave 24:

>   EDWARD L. GRANT
>   CAPT. 307 INF. 77 DIV.
>   NEW YORK, OCT. 5, 1918

A panel in the welcome center honors Grant with a large photo from his baseball days. Other Americans are highlighted as well in rotating panels, including Private Henry Johnson, a member of the Harlem Hellfighters. African-American soldiers fought with the 369th French Regiment, as their white countrymen refused to fight with Black soldiers. In hand-to-hand combat, Johnson was wounded fighting Germans troops in the Argonne. The French government awarded him the Croix de Guerre. He survived to return to the States, but his life after the war was difficult. Despite his decorations for bravery, in 1929 Henry Johnson died in poverty. He was buried in Arlington National Cemetery. Johnson was posthumously awarded the Medal of Honor in 2015 by President Barack Obama, nearly a century after his extraordinary exploits.

SACRIFICE

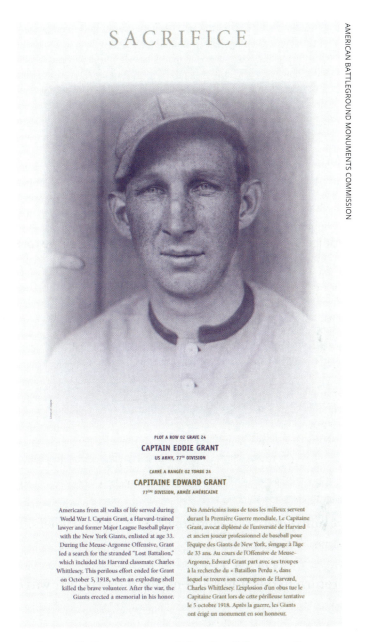

PLOT A ROW 02 GRAVE 24
CAPTAIN EDDIE GRANT
US ARMY, 77ᵀᴴ DIVISION

CARRÉ A RANGÉE 02 TOMBE 24
CAPITAINE EDWARD GRANT
77ᴵᴹᴱ DIVISION, ARMÉE AMÉRICAINE

Americans from all walks of life served during World War I. Captain Grant, a Harvard-trained lawyer and former Major League Baseball player with the New York Giants, enlisted at age 33. During the Meuse-Argonne Offensive, Grant led a search for the stranded "Lost Battalion," which included his Harvard classmate Charles Whittlesey. This perilous effort ended for Grant on October 5, 1918, when an exploding shell killed the brave volunteer. After the war, the Giants erected a memorial in his honor.

Des Américains issus de tous les milieux servent durant la Première Guerre mondiale. Le Capitaine Grant, avocat diplômé de l'université de Harvard et ancien joueur professionnel de baseball pour l'équipe des Giants de New York, s'engage à l'âge de 33 ans. Au cours de l'Offensive de Meuse-Argonne, Edward Grant part avec ses troupes à la recherche du « Bataillon Perdu », dans lequel se trouve son compagnon de Harvard, Charles Whittlesey. L'explosion d'un obus tue le Capitaine Grant lors de cette périlleuse tentative le 5 octobre 1918. Après la guerre, les Giants ont érigé un monument en son honneur.

Edward Grant panel in the Meuse-Argonne American Cemetery Visitor Center

Henry Johnson panel in the Meuse-Argonne American Cemetery Visitor Center

Croix de Guerre, France's highest military honor

CHAPTER VIII

THE PANDEMIC AND OTHER TRAGEDIES

Might illness have taken Grant's life had the shrapnel not killed him first? The first week of September 1918 saw a deadly outbreak of influenza in the U.S. 1st Army. The pandemic was known by various names, but most often, and erroneously, as the Spanish flu. The virus would spread worldwide and kill more people than the war. It was particularly virulent among young, otherwise healthy men. We do know that Grant was terribly ill at the time he fought to rescue the Lost Battalion, so sick he had difficulty holding a coffee cup.

The pandemic that began in 1918 and persisted throughout the next year was the worst in history, affecting a third of the world's population. Estimates of the dead ranged as high as 50 million. There was no known cure. Death came quickly and painfully, as the virus morphed into bacterial pneumonia, especially in the confined quarters of army barracks.

Not everyone who contracted influenza died. General Pershing was likely stricken during the early days of September 1918, when he was exhorting the American Expeditionary Force to continue its drive in the Argonne Forest. During the first week of October, doctors identified 15,000 soldiers of the AEF with influenza.

On the home front, estimates of pandemic deaths ranged from 650,000 to 700,000 and strangely, very little news circulated about the disease. President Woodrow Wilson, who became ill during the peace talks at Versailles, never talked publicly about the pandemic during the war. Newspapers focused instead on what was to be the war's final offensive. Nevertheless, numerous rumors circulated about German espionage and one unproven conspiracy theory was that the pandemic was a German plot.

Public health authorities in a few cities, most notably San Francisco, tried to get people to wear masks and warned about congregating in large numbers. Nurses there exhorted people to wear face masks in public, but the available masks were made of porous gauze that offered little protection.

The pandemic also weakened the German army in its final offensive, and contributed to the myth that a strong Germany had been "stabbed in the back" and had never lost the war. That often-repeated belief in Germany supported Hitler's rise to power in 1933. Most German troops were unaware that the war was winding down and that they were losing. In the fall of 1918, there were negotiations behind the scenes with President Wilson for an armistice, but the fighting remained as brutal as ever.

Numerous professional baseball players were stricken by the flu, most stateside. The first military base affected was Camp Funston at Fort Riley, Kansas. Then Fort Dix in New Jersey was especially hard hit. Among the recruits who died there was Negro League star Tim

Kimbro. Pearl Franklin "Specks" Webster, another standout Negro League player, trained at Fort Dix, but died of influenza in France five days after the war ended. When professional baseball resumed in 1919, one reason the spitball was prohibited was the fear that it would spread influenza. Pershing, in his memoir, wrote about the 16,000 cases of influenza in just one week ending on October 5. As it happened, Eddie Grant was killed that day. In all, 70,000 soldiers were treated for the flu, and many developed pneumonia. Grant likely had both. An astounding number died of their illnesses.

Accidents claimed the lives of many Americans, especially those who volunteered to fly planes, a new and risky weapon of war. They served in the Army Air Service. The Air Service as a separate branch was not created until 1947. Their number included Alexander "Tom" Burr who died in a training exercise while serving in France. Burr had played in just one major league game, as a Yankee in 1914 against the Washington Senators.

The death of Eddie Grant, always a popular teammate, greatly affected New York Giants catcher John "Chief" Meyers, Christy Mathewson's battery mate. A Dartmouth educated Native American from California, Meyers, like Grant, played under John McGraw, and after Grant's death enlisted in the Marine Corps. It is noteworthy that many of the baseball players of the World War I era who had enlisted were college graduates. In addition to "Harvard Eddie" Grant, they included Christy Mathewson, a Bucknell alumnus, Lieutenant Alexander "Tom" Burr, like Charles Whittlesey, a Williams graduate and Branch Rickey, an alumnus of Ohio Wesleyan and the University of Michigan Law School. Only a fair major league catcher, Rickey, as general manager would become famous for signing Jackie Robinson to the Brooklyn Dodgers after World War II, beginning the integration of major league baseball.

The best-known ballplayer in World War I was pitcher Christy Mathewson. At the time Mathewson entered service, he was the manager of the Cincinnati Reds. At the end of 1918, Mathewson crossed the Atlantic to join the Army of Occupation, becoming terribly seasick en route. He was a captain in the Gas and Flame Division of the Army Chemical Warfare Service, as were Branch Rickey and the "Georgia Peach" Ty Cobb. During a training exercise, Mathewson came into contact with mustard gas that damaged his lungs. He survived the accident, but in 1925, still a young man, Mathewson died of tuberculosis. The future Hall of Famer was a late casualty of war. Less well-known was pitcher Anthony Mahoney who played for three different teams in the Negro Leagues and sickened after a gas attack in France. He succumbed to his injuries in 1924. Two other professional baseball players died in service shoreside. Weakened in the worldwide influenza outbreak, Larry Chappell succumbed to pneumonia in 1918. Chappell had played for five seasons on three teams beginning in 1913. Another player, Newt Halliday, died of pneumonia at the Great Lakes Naval Station. He had played in a single game with the Pittsburgh Pirates in 1916.

The Covid pandemic a century later was first identified at the very end of 2019, and quickly spread worldwide. It reached the United States in January 2020, and remarkably in the summer of 2021, the Food and Drug Administration (FDA) approved a vaccine. Of course, a century earlier, with no vaccines, the so-called Spanish Flu was clinically untreatable. In the United States, the death toll was lower in 1919 than it was in the twenty-first century Covid pandemic.

CHAPTER IX

THE MYSTERY

On Decoration Day, May 30, 1921, between games of a doubleheader at the Polo Grounds with the Philadelphia Phillies, the New York Giants dedicated a plaque in deepest centerfield honoring Eddie Grant. Bronze and weighing about 75 pounds, the plaque was secured to a five-foot block of granite. The solemn occasion was attended by soldiers, baseball notables, a Harvard representative, and Eddie Grant's two sisters, Louise and Florence. The monument reads:

> In Memory of Capt. Edward Leslie Grant
> 307th Infantry 77th Division
> AEF
> Soldier Scholar Athlete
> Killed in Action
> Argonne Forest
> October 5, 1918
> Erected by Friends in Baseball Journalism and the Service

It also listed the teams that Grant played for and the dates: Philadelphia Nationals, 1907, 1908, 1909, 1910; Cincinnati Reds, 1911, 1912, 1913; New York Giants, 1913, 1914, 1915. There were eight teams in each league, and Grant played for three of them in the National League.

One of the journalists who was especially moved by Grant's heroic story was Grantland Rice, the most celebrated sportswriter of the first half of the 20th century. He had enlisted in the army in 1917, at the age of 38, and during the war was on the editorial staff of *Stars and Stripes*, published in Paris for the American Expeditionary Force in the years 1918 and 1919. Rice is best known for immortalizing the backfield of the Notre Dame football team as "The Four Horsemen of the Apocalypse".

Rice wrote a poem memorializing Eddie Grant on the occasion of the dedication of the memorial:

CAPTAIN EDWARD LESLIE GRANT

Killed in Action-the Argonne – October 5th, 1918.

Far from the Game and the cheering of old,
A cross in the Argonne will tell you the story
Where each one may read on its rain-battered mold
A final box score that is written in glory.
The final box score of a Player who gave
The flag that he fought for, his ghost - and his grave.

Green be his couch where the white lilies lean.
Crimson the poppies that keep guard above him.
Gentle the darkness that gathers between
The Player at rest and the torn hearts that love him.
God give him refuge where Life's flag is furled,
A dreamer gone back to the dust of the world.

Low be the lost winds of France that must creep
Over his rest in the Last Tavern lying.
God send Thy dreams where the Darkness is deep,
Father, thy care when the wild storms are flying.
No monarch there - but the soul of a Man -
We speak for a Brother - for One of the Clan!

— GRANTLAND RICE

The Grant monument in the Polo Grounds was in front of the 483-foot marker. On rare times when balls were hit into the farthest reaches of the deep outfield, radio broadcasters often referred to the plaque that honored the former infielder. There were other plaques, John McGraw's for example, but they were on the clubhouse wall. Grant's was the only one on the field.

Ceremony to place Grant plaque on the field in the Polo Grounds

After the dedication, there was a ceremony every Decoration Day (officially renamed Memorial Day in 1967). In the years following the dedication of the memorial, a few followed the lead of Grantland Rice and worked to keep the memory of Harvard Eddie alive. There were occasional articles in newspapers on anniversaries of Grant's passing, especially during World War ll.

In the 1920s, there was talk of renaming Braves Field, home of the National League Boston team, for Grant. And some sportswriters championed Eddie Grant's admission into the Hall of Fame in Cooperstown. Nothing came of either idea. There is a replica plaque outside the Giants' home field in San Francisco, now Oracle Park. Today most Americans, including most Giant fans, do not know about Eddie Grant. There is a famous photograph of Willie Mays going deep in the outfield of the Polo Grounds to make that iconic catch of a long drive hit by Vic Wertz of the Cleveland Indians in the first game of the 1954 World Series. The Grant monument is clearly visible on the left side of the photograph.

Willie Mays and Grant's plaque on the left of the photo

On the last day that the New York Giants played in the Polo Grounds before leaving New York for San Francisco, fans trashed the ballpark. The *New York Times* reported on September 30, 1957 that fans vented their emotions by chasing the players off the field and making souvenirs out of the stadium:

> The bases, home plate, and pitching rubber were torn up. The bullpen sun shield was smashed, and patches of outfield grass ripped out. Even telephones and phonebooks were looted. The mass pursuit was touched off by affection, excitement, nostalgia, curiosity, and annoyance at the fact that the team will represent San Francisco.

The Grant plaque disappeared, reportedly pried off its granite block by three rampaging teens. From time to time a few baseball insiders noted its disappearance. The Polo Grounds itself was razed in 1964. On its site, the city built a public housing project fittingly named Polo Grounds Towers.

In the years following the move of the Giants to San Francisco, rumors occasionally surfaced about the whereabouts of the plaque. Baseball buffs generally agree on two points: that teenage boys ran off with the plaque, and that policemen on duty at the Polo Grounds took it away from them. And then its whereabouts became a mystery.

The theories about its disappearance include the following: that three drunken reporters brought the Grant plaque to Toots Shor's Restaurant, a watering hole in Manhattan. According to this account, Shor, a noted sports fan, who famously called himself "a saloon keeper," turned it over to an American Legion post. But there were two posts named for Grant, and neither one has it, nor, it appears, do any other posts.

The most repeated theory perhaps, is a bogus story that the new owner of a house in Ho Ho Kus, New Jersey, found the plaque in his attic some forty years after the original was stolen from the Polo Grounds. According to the story, the house had belonged to a New York City policeman, one who was at the Polo Grounds on the day of the last Giants' home game in New York. The owner, so goes the story, an attorney, was unaware of the significance of the plaque, and made inquiries from friends. Eventually, Albert Kilchesty, an archivist in California, was contacted, and plans were made to ship the plaque to Pasadena. The recipients were Kilchesty and Terry Cannon, a baseball enthusiast and founder of The Baseball Reliquary, a repository of odd baseball paraphernalia. Terry Cannon in letters hinted that this was all a spoof, sometimes intimating that the plaque that he had was a replica. The Reliquary exhibited baseball cards and other memorabilia but had no official home. The Grant plaque would be an important addition to the collection. While the men waited to exhibit it, it was kept in the garage of a home belonging to Cannon and his wife Mary.

According to Kilchesty, the men secured a perfect space to show their collection, an empty library building in Pomona, California. With a great deal of effort, they managed to haul the heavy plaque into the trunk of their car and headed to the library. After they had emptied the car of all its contents, but not the trunk, an alert librarian noticed that the trunk was open. The men went to investigate and found that the plaque had been stolen.

A letter signed by Terry Cannon about the theft of the Grant plaque stated that it was stolen on Sunday, April 1, 2001. April first is April Fool's Day! That was a hint. So was the town where it was presumably found, Ho Ho Kus, a real place, but with a name that suggested that this was a hoax. Still, the story has been repeated innumerable times. Albert Kilchesty, admitting to the ruse, believes that the plaque may still be hiding in plain view behind a bar somewhere in New Jersey. It might be, the mystery remains.

The San Francisco Giants erected a new plaque and placed it outside of the stadium in a rather obscure corner. Perhaps for some in the San Francisco Giants organization, Eddie Grant was a player for the New York Giants, and less meaningful to the team on the West

Coast. Certainly, not everyone felt that way, and that plaque was commissioned in 2007 "by friends in baseball, journalism and the service" as was the original.

In the Bronx, Edward L. Grant Highway is a few blocks north of Yankee Stadium, just off Jerome Avenue in the western part of the borough. Dean College in Grant's hometown of Franklin, Massachusetts, has a ballfield named for Grant. There were also American Legion Posts in New York and Boston named for him as well as a World War II Liberty ship, the *SS Edward L. Grant,* launched on June 12, 1943.

Still, Eddie Grant remains largely unknown to the general public. If the original memorial plaque were to surface it would be newsworthy, and perhaps the current generation of baseball fans would learn about the courageous soldier who gave his life in the service of his country.

Liberty ship SS Edward L. Grant

CHAPTER X

THE 1918 WORLD SERIES AND CONTEMPORARY SUBJECTS

Eddie Grant, despite his focus on the war, would have taken an interest in the 1918 World Series between the Boston Red Sox and the Chicago Cubs, the only one ever played entirely in the month of September. The baseball season was shortened due to the war. He also might have been interested in the fact that the Red Sox were playing close enough to Franklin Massachusetts to be his home team. Although Grant played professionally almost exclusively on National League teams, he could have been rooting for an American League win. He did begin his major league career in 1905 with the Cleveland Naps, but in fact, had played in just two American League games.

The 1918 series was notable for many reasons. Playing for the Red Sox, Babe Ruth pitched and won two games, and he began a streak of 29.2 scoreless innings pitched in a World Series. That was only broken by Whitey Ford of the Yankees in 1961. Ruth hit a triple but no home runs. In fact, neither did any other player on either the winning Boston Red Sox or the losing Chicago Cubs. A World Series with no home runs was a first and never repeated phenomenon. After the 1919 season, Babe Ruth was sold to the rival New York Yankees, giving rise to the "Curse of the Bambino" a Red Sox streak of not winning a World Series until 2004.

Due to patriotic sentiments engendered by the war, it was the first time that the Star-Spangled Banner was played at a major league game. The Cubs were the first team to play it during the seventh-inning stretch and it was repeated throughout the series. The Star-Spangled Banner, however, did not become the national anthem until 1931.

The final game of the six-game 1918 World Series was played on September 11, and would have been reported in *Stars and Stripes* and *The Sporting News* and avidly followed by American troops in Europe. Surely Grant would have been one of those fans. Grant wrote his last letter home on August 31, just five days before the start of the 1918 World Series.

PREPAREDNESS

The United States was not prepared for war. Grant interrupted his legal career in 1917, volunteering to train as an officer at Camp Plattsburgh in upstate New York. He was in the company of many Harvard graduates who believed in the importance of the preparedness movement. Along with other college-educated young men, he followed the lead of Theodore Roosevelt and Roosevelt's Rough Rider commander, Dr. Leonard Wood. Roosevelt wrote derisively of Woodrow Wilson who ran on the 1916 Democratic platform to keep the United States out of war. In a speech the same year, TR said, "Instead of speaking softly and carrying a big stick, President Wilson spoke bombastically and carried a dishrag." Pacifists and others opposing the preparedness movement from the start of the Great War in 1914, worked to keep the United States out of the fighting. They included Henry Ford who financed the voyage of the Oscar II Peace Ship, an unsuccessful expedition in 1914. It was led by Rosika Schwimmer, a Hungarian refugee, to bring peace to Europe. Critics called it the "ship of fools."

WOMEN SUFFRAGE

A headline-making issue during Eddie Grant's life was the fight for the Nineteenth Amendment to give women the right to vote. Grant did not live to see its passage, proposed on June 4, 1919, and ratified on August 18, 1920. Grant was a devotee of Theodore Roosevelt, and Roosevelt, at least after his time as president had been outspoken in his support of women suffrage. Roosevelt first publicly supported the right of women to vote in 1912, when he was a losing candidate for president on the Progressive (Bull Moose Party) ticket. In 1914, he appeared with the president of the American Woman Suffrage Association, Rev. Anna Howard Shaw, demonstrating his support for women suffrage.

On the subject of the suffrage, Woodrow Wilson initially opposed the right of women to vote. It is rather ironic that the Nineteenth Amendment passed in the last year of his presidency. President Wilson only agreed to the amendment after strong tactics by women, including a highly publicized hunger strike. It forced Wilson to reverse his position. Theodore Roosevelt detested Woodrow Wilson, a Democrat, calling him "the most wretched creature we have had in the Presidential chair." Eddie Grant and his class of young men, almost all Republicans, would likely have followed Roosevelt and his support for women's suffrage.

IMMIGRATION

What can be surmised about Eddie Grant's attitude to the large influx of immigrants in the early twentieth century?

Theodore Roosevelt had talked derisively about "hyphenated Americans." However, he also wrote, "There are good men and bad men of all nationalities, creeds, and colors; and if this world of ours is ever to become what we hope someday it may become, it must be by a general recognition that the man's heart and soul, the man's worth and actions, determine his standing." Eddie Grant's 77th was largely made up of immigrants, those so-called "hyphenated Americans."

"Half-Americans" was a term Germans used to describe captured American soldiers of German descent, who surprised their captors by their loyalty to America. Nevertheless, immigrants were belittled by some prominent Americans, such as the powerful chairman of the Senate Foreign Relations Committee, Senator Henry Cabot Lodge of Massachusetts, a close ally of Theodore Roosevelt. We do know that Grant's men thought highly of him, his determination, and his fighting spirit, even when exhausted and sick on the final day of his life. As a ballplayer, Harvard Eddie was a team player and disposed to work for a common goal with all those around him.

MUSIC

The anthem of baseball, "Take Me Out to the Ballgame" was written in 1908 when Eddie Grant was playing for the Phillies. While the song was popular during Eddie Grant's life, surprisingly it was not played in a World Series until 1934 in the fourth game between the St. Louis Cardinals and the Detroit Tigers. Cardinal pitchers, brothers Paul and Dizzy Dean each won two games in a series that the Cardinals won in seven.

When Grant was in college, jazz became the rage. Evolved from the ragtime of the 1890s, it was created by African-Americans and spread throughout the nation. The best-known performer was Scott Joplin, composer of "Maple Leaf Rag" (1899), "The Entertainer" (1902), and dozens of other ragtime compositions. Joplin died in 1917, at the age of 48. Americans also knew the music of John Philip Sousa, especially his marches. Best known were "Semper Fidelis," (1888) the official march of the U.S. Marine Corps, and his most enduring composition, "Stars and Stripes Forever" (1896). Bands played Sousa's music on national holidays and in school assemblies across the United States

A joyful form of staged entertainment in Eddie Grant's lifetime was vaudeville, and the most popular vaudevillian and Broadway star was George M. Cohan. Cohan wrote Yankee Doodle Dandy in 1904 and sang it on Broadway in the musical "Little Johnny Jones." Two years later, he published "You're a Grand Old Flag," and in 1917 he wrote "Over There," the inspiring World War I call to arms. A popular song in the first decade of the 20th century was Billy Murray's recording of "In My Merry Oldsmobile," with its famous line - "Come away with me Lucille in my merry Oldsmobile…." Did Eddie Grant drive; did he have a car? I wish I knew.

APPENDIX

THE UNITED STATES 1883 - 1918
THE LIFESPAN OF EDDIE GRANT

From the time of Eddie Grant's birth in 1883 to his death in 1918, the United States changed dramatically. Eddie Grant's early years coincided with the Gilded Age, an era of great wealth for the few, and grinding poverty for many. Mark Twain's novel, *The Gilded Age*, which so aptly gave its name to the era, was published just 10 years before Eddie Grant was born. It was a time of unprecedented industrial growth spurred by extraordinary genius.

John D. Rockefeller monopolized the oil business. Andrew Carnegie dominated the steel industry. J.P. Morgan, the leading financier of his day, created the first billion-dollar corporation. Railroad barons made great fortunes while linking the nation. Beginning in Manhattan in 1887, Thomas Edison lit streets that were dark after sunset. Three days after Eddie Grant's birth, the Brooklyn Bridge opened, connecting Manhattan and Brooklyn. New York City in 1883 had over a million inhabitants, the only American city with a population that exceeded a million. Philadelphia was the second-largest city, and Brooklyn, not yet part of New York City, was third. Brooklyn would merge with New York City in 1898.

In the decade of the 1880s, more than five million people entered the country from abroad. These immigrants built the nation's railroads and worked steel mills and oil fields. Most passed by the welcoming lady in the harbor erected in 1886, later giving its nickname to Grant's 77th, the Statue of Liberty Division.

There were 37 states in the United States in 1883, and every major city was east of the Mississippi River. Much of the west was still in territorial stages. The president of the United States was Chester A. Arthur, a Republican politician who, as vice president, became president when James Garfield, was assassinated in the first year of his presidency. The population of the United States was about fifty million in 1883. In just thirty-five years, the number of years that Eddie Grant lived, the population of the United States doubled to a hundred million people. Millions of hopeful immigrants came to America. The influx created controversial issues in the early years of the twentieth century. To make new lives for themselves, Irish, Greeks, Italians, Poles, Russians, and many others - Catholics and Jews - were entering a largely Protestant country. At the time of Grant's death in 1918, there were forty-eight states in the continental United States. The last of the forty-eight to join the union was Arizona in 1912. Alaska and Hawaii became states in 1959.

Germany surrendered on November 11, 1918, on the basis of Wilson's Fourteen Points. Eddie Grant had died just five weeks earlier. Woodrow Wilson led a delegation to Versailles, France in 1919 that redrew the map of Europe to conform, to the extent practical, to the self-determination of nationalities. The United States never became a signatory to the Treaty of Versailles as the Senate refused to ratify it. The United States did not assume a position commensurate with its power at the end of the war, for during the Great War, the United States had surpassed Great Britain as the world's richest and most powerful nation. America had come of age but was slow to assume the mantle of leadership.

VITAL STATISTICS OF THE 77TH DIVISION

TOTAL CASUALTIES OF THE 77TH DIVISION

	Officers	Men
Killed in Action	69	1299
Died of Wounds Received in Action	10	188
Severely Wounded	69	1894
Slightly Wounded	82	2889
Gassed	71	2297
Missing	13	696
Prisoners	3	31
TOTAL	317	9294

Note: Approximately 7500 sick, evacuated to hospitals, not included in above totals.

Total casualties approximately 17,000

THE HISTORY OF THE 77TH DIVISION (AUG. 25, 1917 – NOV. 11, 1918)

LETTER FROM EDDIE GRANT TO HIS SISTER

Dear Florence,

I am an applicant for a commission in the Officer's Reserve Corps as you will see in a letter to father. The marital spirit of the Grants was bound to assert itself. But!! – don't allow Earle to get foolish. There are enough fellows in my position without others – he can do twice as much good right where he is.

I cannot make this too strong – his garden and work is enough. I want also to enforce upon you that I am not the least bit pessimistic about this and can't see why any of you should be. Why, these Germans won't be able to win a game from us. We would knock old Hinderburg (sic) out of the box in the first inning.

There are several of us in this house who are applying – maybe also probably all will not be accepted. McCormick my roommate (formerly) is among them. He took his physical exam yesterday and had an accident – for when they took his chest expansion – he broke the tape measure. He expanded seven inches.

Well, will write anon and let them all know that if necessary, I will do all the fighting for all of us. But don't think it will be necessary.

With love,
Les.

> Franklin Mass
> Dec 29th 1918
>
> Mr. William C Lane
> Librarian Harvard College Library.
>
> My Dear Sir
>
> I was very sorry I did not meet you on Saturday as I should liked very much to have explained to you about my Sons Death. However all I can say that Capt Edward L. Grant of the 307 (Reg. Inf. Division) was Killed in Action Oct 9th 1918 while leading his Division to the relief of the Lost Battalion in Argonne Forrest. I am sending you a clipping from the Stars & Stripes a paper printed over there. I also had a letter from the Surgeon who was with him and he says that he was buried nicely. he himself putting some sods around the Grave. I thank you very much for your Interest in my Sons Death
>
> Yours very tr.
> Geo H. Grant

Note wrong date of Grant's death in the letter Eddie Grant's father wrote to the librarian at the Harvard College Library written several months after his son's death.

Aug. 31, 1918

Dear Father: —

Have not had much chance to write lately but take the time to tell you that I am all right — even if I am very dirty — have no clothes and need a haircut. My trousers were fine until the other day when I ripped them rolling over the edge of a sunken road to avoid a playful shell they fired at me and an automatic gunner as we were coming across the fields. We soon were under cover but my last pair of trousers were spoiled and cant see just when will get another pair for stores are rather scarce over here.

Fall is in the air here and guess it sets in rather early — but hear that it does not get so

cold as it does in New
Hampshire for instance.
    Just now we are resting
a little - in fact just beginning
it and we all hope that
it will continue for some
time as we are all rather
tired - We have not had
much sleep lately and the
thing that bothered the men
most was that for five days
they had nothing but canned
beef and crackers they now
have hot coffee but now

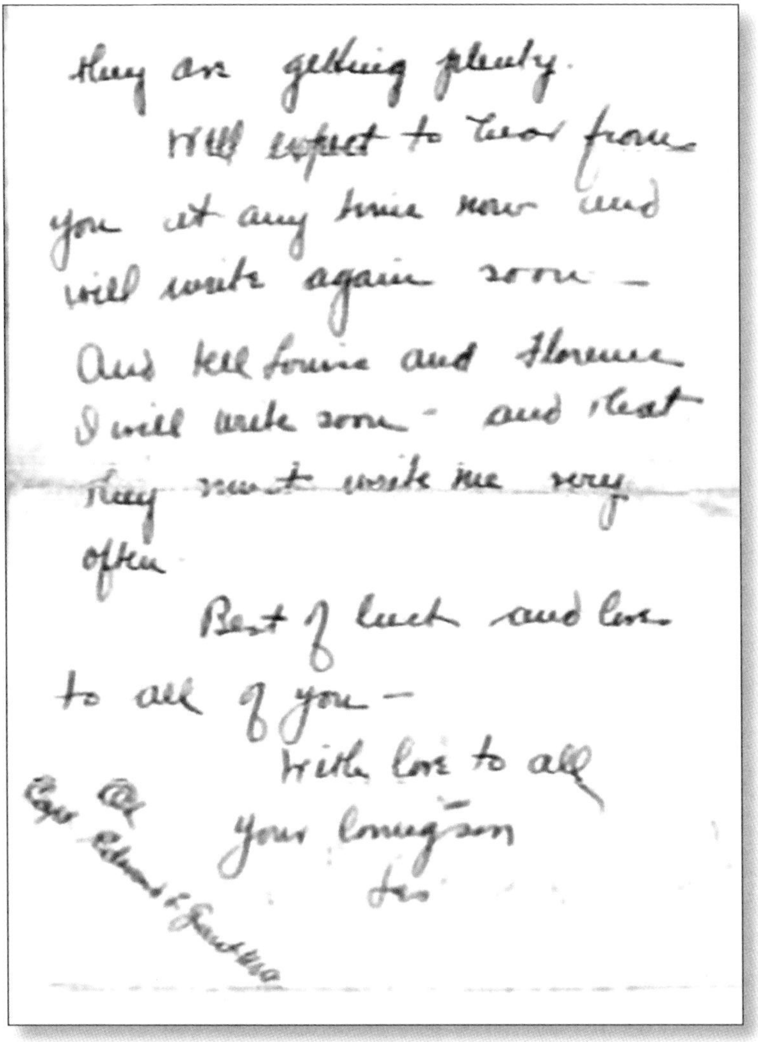

they are getting plenty.

Will expect to hear from you at any time now and will write again soon —

And tell Louise and Florence I will write soon - and that they must write me very often

Best of luck and love to all of you —

With love to all
Your loving son
Ed

Capt Edward L Grant USA

KAREN KUBALA

Handwritten letter from Eddie Grant to his father

Author in the Argonne Forest

FOR FURTHER READING

Barbeau, Arthur E. and Florette Henri. *The Unknown Soldiers: Black American Troops in World War I*. Philadelphia, Temple University Press, 1974.

Beschloss, Michael. *Presidents of War*. Crown, New York, 2018.

Carroll, Andrew. *My Fellow Soldiers: General John Pershing and the Americans Who Helped Win the Great War*. New York, Penguin Random House, New York, 2018.

Deford, Frank. *The Old Ball Game: How John McGraw, Christy Mathewson, and the New York Giants Created Modern Baseball*. Grove Press, New York, 2005.

Goldberger, Paul. *Baseball in the American City*. Alfred A. Knopf, New York, 2020.

History of the Seventy Seventh Division: August 25. 1917 - November 11th, 1918. 77th Division Association, New York, 1919.

Keegan, John. *The First World War*. Alfred A. Knopf, New York, 1999.

Kershaw, Ian. *To Hell and Back: Europe 1914-1949*. Penguin, New York, 2015.

Lanning, Michael Lee. *The African American Soldier: A Two-Hundred Year History of African-Americans in the U.S. Military*. Citadel Press, New York, 2004,

Lears, Jackson. *The Making of Modern America, 1877-1920*. Harper Perennial, New York, 2009.

Marshall, S.L.A. *World War I*. Houghton Mifflin, New York, 1964.

Posnanski, Joe. *The Baseball 100*. Avid Reader Press, New York, 2021.

Putnam, William Lowell. *The Kaiser's Merchant Ships in World War I*. McFarland and Co., Jefferson, N.C., 2001.

Ritter, Lawrence S. *The Glory of Their Times: The Story of the Early Days of Baseball*. Harper Perennial, New York, 1992.

Robinson, Ray. *Matty An American Hero: Christy Mathewson of the New York Giants*. Oxford University Press, New York, 1993.

Rubin, Richard. *The Last of the Doughboys: The Forgotten Generation and Their Forgotten World War*. Houghton Mifflin Harcourt, New York, 2013.

_____. *Back Over There*. St. Martin's Press, New York, 2017.

Rudd, Daniel. *Theodore Roosevelt's History of the United States: His Own Words*. Harper, New York, 2010.

Shah, Sonia. *Pandemic*. Farrar, Straus and Giroux, New York, 2016.

Tuchman, Barbara. *The Guns of August*. Macmillan, New York, 1962.

New York Herald, Tuesday, October 22, 1918

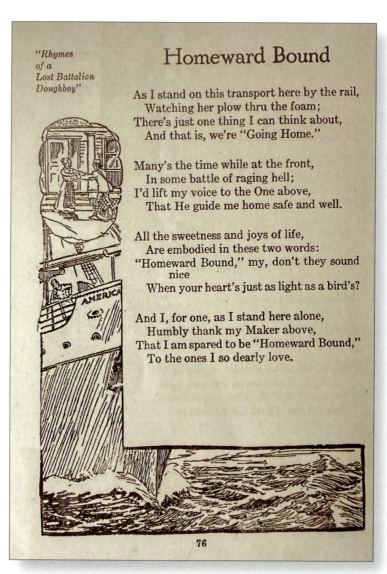

"Rhymes of a Lost Battalion Doughboy"

Homeward Bound

As I stand on this transport here by the rail,
    Watching her plow thru the foam;
There's just one thing I can think about,
    And that is, we're "Going Home."

Many's the time while at the front,
    In some battle of raging hell;
I'd lift my voice to the One above,
    That He guide me home safe and well.

All the sweetness and joys of life,
    Are embodied in these two words:
"Homeward Bound," my, don't they sound nice
    When your heart's just as light as a bird's?

And I, for one, as I stand here alone,
    Humbly thank my Maker above,
That I am spared to be "Homeward Bound,"
    To the ones I so dearly love.

from History and Rhymes of the Lost Battalion by "Buck Private" McCollum

EDDIE GRANT, FIRST BALL-PLAYER KILLED

EDDIE GRANT IN ACTION

adhere to the things they know. The Basques are successful in commerce and in letters, but the Bretons are medieval.

The French-Canadians are the most backward people on the North American Continent. They still use wooden plows, though living among the most advanced and progressive people in the world. Their customs are those of the middle ages. They are fine, strong folk, love their homes, have large families and abominate change. Not a hopeful people for propaganda.

The French temperament is better suited to baseball than that of the British, but I look for Evers to attain his greatest success among the Australians and New Zealanders. These are new peoples, and inclined to adopt new things. They have work to do and no time for cricket, which requires a week to play.

Mathewson's trip to France meant more to him than the overseas journey means to most men who have made it.

PHOTO BY DIANE SOLON

ABOUT THE AUTHOR

Historian Karen Fox Markoe is a Distinguished Professor at the State University of New York Maritime College. For thirty years, she has been chairperson of its humanities department. A graduate of Hunter College, she earned both a master's in Modern European History and a Ph.D. in American History from Columbia University.

A daughter of the Bronx and a lifelong Yankees fan, Professor Markoe is married to Arnold Markoe, Professor Emeritus, Brooklyn College. They are the parents of two daughters, Lauren and Nancy, and grandparents of four grandchildren, Aaron, Rachel, Zachary, and Jacob.